2 ◀ RUP100

D1015156

# #prehistoric
## FOLLOW THE DINOSAURS

Scholastic Inc.

**28**
photos

**310**
followers

**90,026**
following

Author: JOHN OWE

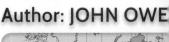

Los
Ange

The publisher does not have any control over and does not assume any responsibili
for author or third-party websites or their content.

This book is a work of fiction. Names, characters, places, and incidents are either th
product of the author's imagination or are used fictitiously, and any resemblanc
to actual persons, living or dead, business establishments, events, websites, onlin
identifiers, or references (e.g., URL, email address, username, hashtag) or locales i
entirely coincidental.

ISBN 978-0-545-75164-3

10 9 8 7 6 5 4 3 2 1          15 16 17 18 19

Printed in the U.S.A. 40
First edition, January 2015
Book design by Jessica Meltzer

# TABLEOFCONTENTS

# #prehistoric
## FOLLOW THE DINOSAURS

1
photos

0
followers

0
following

North
Ameri

Username: INTERRUPTINGDINO
Name: Iguanodon (iguana tooth)
Period: Cretaceous (135–125 million years ago)
Size: 30 feet long, 16 feet tall – with 6-inch spikes on my thum
Diet: Plants 4 lyfe 🙄
Hangouts: North America, North Africa, Europe
Bio: WHOOHOO FIRST DINO ON HERE!! I'm about that selfie
life. Right now, I'm all by my selfie. #irock #iroll #irule

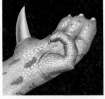

⭐ 59 LOVES

HELLO! WELCOME! I have an absolutely ENORMOUS announcement! That's right . . . I am #THRILLED to announce . . . THAT I JUST TOOK THIS SELFIE!! #BOOM! #INSTADINO! #SUPERCOOL! #PrehistoryInTheMaking!

 **INTERRUPTINGDINO** Yello? #partyof1

**132** photos

**1,000** followers

**1.2M** following

Ancie
Ocea
Floor

Username: TRILL_O_BYTE

Name: Trilobite (three-lobed)

Period: Cambrian through the Permian (541–251 million years
ago . . . What about you? Oh, you've been around for 8–12 yea
Nice! You've only got, what, 270,999,992 years to go?!)

Size: One trilobite. I ran the scene for such a long time that I do
really measure myself by anyone else's standards.

Diet: Delicious, nutritious scum. Yum!

Hangouts: The floors of every ancient ocean.

Bio: I'm one of the most numerous animals in the ancient seas.
And, oh, as if that weren't "enough"? Well, ever heard of insects
Oh, you have? I'm an early ancestor to all of them. #ThatsTrill

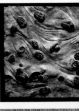

★ 201 LOVES

Hang time with my clique. Bffs #4lyfe #Byte4eva

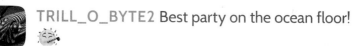

TRILL_O_BYTE2 Best party on the ocean floor! 🐡

TRILL_O_BYTE5 We takin' over!! 😎

TRILL_O_BYTE VIT* ONLY! *(very important trilobites)!

**15**
photos

**105**
followers

**372**
following

Shallo
Seas N
Europ

Username: TERRORGOTYA
Name: Pterygotus (wing-animal)
Period: Silurian (443–419 million years ago)
Size: 7 feet 4 inches
Diet: Anything in the sea. Watch out!
Hangouts: Shallow seas of North America/Europe
Bio: I'm a #SeaScorpion. Wait, you guys don't have those anymore? Are you sure? I mean, I was really scary and successf for my time. I feel like I would have stuck around. Oh! Wait! Maybe I turned invisible so that I could be even more deadly. Yeah, that must be what happened.

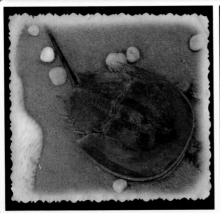

⭐ **44 LOVES**

Claw party! #ancientinsectancestor #fearsomepredator #killerinstinct

 **@HORSESHOECRAB** Hey, buddy. Saw your "about me" section. Don't worry, man! I'm your descendant.

 **TERRORGOTYA** PHEW, @HorseshoeCrab. 😀 I knew we couldn't just be GONE. Wow, a crab the size of a horse! My relatives are huge! Let me just click on your link to see how big you guys really are. WAIT . . . WHAT THE?!!?!

| 21 photos |
| 707 followers |
| 291 following |

Morocc

**Username:** DUNKLE_BONE
**Name:** Dunkleosteus ("Dunkle's bone." Your guess is as good as mine there. If I ever meet the guy who named me . . . Let's just s I'm going to bite him with my #hugejaws.)
**Period:** Devonian (374–360 million years ago)
**Size:** Bigger than a great white shark
**Diet:** Carnivore (I had a bite MORE powerful than a great white.)
**Hangouts:** Morocco, Belgium, Poland, North America
**Bio:** I'm an armor-plated fish and the greatest predator of my time. I was the biggest animal ever before the dinosaurs came along. Gosh, I'd like to bite them. #soreloser

⭐ **122 LOVES**

Say cheese! #badtothebone #strongbite #SchoolBusSized

 **OFFICIAL_REX1** Did somebody say bite?

 **DUNKLE_BONE** @Official_Rex1 I'm not scared of you! My bite is as strong as yours! 😬

**52**
photos

**1,054**
followers

**537**
following

Europe

Username: HAIRTIPSFORSHARKS
Name: Stethacanthus (chest spike)
Period: Devonian to Carboniferous (390–360 million years ago
Size: 6 feet long, 100 pounds
Diet: Smaller sharks and other fish
Hangouts: North America, Europe
Bio: As an ancient shark, it's always important to look good. If we're gonna be around for millions of years, we better always look #pictureready. #GetYourHairRight and the #RestWillFollo #wordstoliveby

⭐ **33 LOVES**

Bored with your look? Try a bumpy and toothlike updo! #protip #hair101

**HAMMERHEADHILARY** Having a great hammer day thanks to you @hairtipsforsharks. 🎩

**HAIRTIPSFORSHARKS** Thanks for the love, @hammerheadhilary. Keep checking back for our sharktip swag.

**172** photos

**2,347** followers

**129** following

Northe Canad

Username: ADVENTUROUSAMPHIBIAN

Name: Tiktaalik (the word for a type of fish in the Inuit language used in the territory I was discovered!)

Period: Devonian (375 million years ago)

Size: 10 feet long

Diet: #Surf? Check. #Turf? Check. #NoPickyEatersHere

Hangouts: Nunavut, Northern Canada

Bio: Follow me as I use my primitive legs, primitive lung-like gill and extraordinary bravery to go where no amphibians have gon before!

★ 1 LOVE

Here we are, folks! I am about to attempt to use my #slightlyleglike fins to #push myself onto the #finalfrontier: land! Follow along in the comments below!

 ADVENTUROUSAMPHIBIAN All right! This is it! There's no turning back now. This is #onesmallstep for me, #onegiantleap for future amphibian kind . . .

 ADVENTUROUSAMPHIBIAN . . . AND I'M HERE! I'm up here, in the air! I'm #FLOPPING all around. I look super #awkward.

 ADVENTUROUSAMPHIBIAN And now, #victorious, I will slip back into the water, as any more time up here would #drymeout.

**72** photos
**135** followers
**202** following

North
Americ
Fores

Username: #1_REPTILIA
Name: Hylonomus (forest mouse)
Period: Carboniferous (359–299 million years ago)
Size: 1 foot long, 1 pound
Diet: insects #mmmmm
Hangouts: Forests of North America
Bio: I'm the first modern reptile. That's right – lizards, snakes, an
crocodiles all wish they could be me. Life was hard for a little
while without any friends, but now that I'm on land, I'm living th
good life. #dollabillz #getmoney

⭐ **82 LOVES**

#MovingOnUp. These new #eggs with #shells of mine mean that I can live on land full-time. Now the only time you'll see me by the water's edge is when I'm #catchingsomerays by the pool. #thefinerthings #richreptilesofinstagram

 **ADVENTUROUSAMPHIBIAN** hey @#1_Reptilia where's my #cashmoney? I found that land. #findersfee

**102** photos

**200** followers

**646** following

Wyom[i]

**Username:** SUPADUPAFLY

**Name:** Meganeura

**Period:** Carboniferous (359–299 million years ago)

**Size:** An eagle! (aka I'm absolutely ripped for a bug) #gymtime

**Diet:** Other smaller and weaker insects

**Hangouts:** Wyoming

**Bio:** I'm a griffinfly – the biggest insect of all time. I work hard fo[r] that title, though. I watch what I eat, and I get plenty of exercise[.] Sometimes I fly for hours just working off the protein I had for lunch. Insects are delicious!

⭐ **42 LOVES**

Just KILLED #workoutwednesday. It's official: my wings are #twoandahalffeetlong and now I #ruletheskies.

 **#1_REPTILIA** Mmm, eyes on the flies. #lunch #lookoutbelow

 **SUPADUPAFLY** Watch out, @#1_reptilia. You haven't seen how ripped I am.

**331**
photos

**243**
followers

**176**
following

Israel

**Username:** CAPTAIN_COOLIO
**Name:** Dimetrodon
**Period:** Permian (299–252 million years ago)
**Size:** One 6-foot-3-inch man standing on another 6-foot-3-inc[h] man's shoulders
**Diet:** Carnivore
**Hangouts:** Israel, Germany, Switzerland, China
**Bio:** Awwww, yeah. Here I come! I existed before the dinosaurs and I'm more closely related to mammals! And see that big hum[p] on top of my body? That's called a sail. I guess you could call me the Captain. Captain of cool.

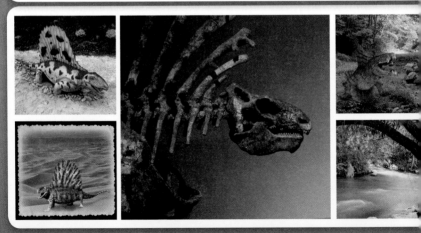

⭐ 1,006 LOVES
Land ahoy! #nosailgotojail  Get it trending, folks! 😎

**DOUBLEDIPPER** That's pretty good. But how about #youhavearuffle #onyourback?

**CAPTAIN_COOLIO** #smh . . . so immature. Stop trolling my account. #coolrules

**772** photos
**401** followers
**393** following

Russ

Username: PROMKING15
Name: Estemmenosuchus
Period: Permian (299–252 million years ago)
Size: 13 feet long, 500 pounds
Diet: Herbivorous
Hangouts: Russia
Bio: My name means "crowned crocodile" –I'm taking that as a great sign for the Permian Prom next week! I'm using this accou to take selfies so that I can be sure I look my best! Since we don have mirrors in the Permian, I've never seen what I look like. I'm almost as excited to see my selfie as I am for prom!

👑
*The Permian Prom*

299–252 million years ago
Russian Countryside
9-12 p.m.

In the event of rain, snow, or the Permian
Extinction, prom will be rescheduled
for a later date.

**13 LOVES**

Okay . . . #testing #testing . . . let's see how this works. All right, taking a #snap of my face. #selfiealert! Now I'll turn this around and finally see just how smokin' hot I really am.  #Three . . . #Two . . . #One . . . and #OHNOOOOOOOOOOOOOOOOOOOOOOOOOOOOOOOOOOOOOOOOOOOOOOOOOOOOOOOOOOOOOOOOOOOOOOOOOOOOOOOOOOOOOOOOOOOOOOOOOOOOOOOOOOOOOOOOOOOOOOOOOOOOOOOOOOO 😨

**101** photos

**494** followers

**881** following

Texa

Username: DOUBLEDIPPER

Name: Diplocaulus

Period: Permian (299–252 million years ago)

Size: 3 feet long

Diet: Insects and fish

Hangouts: Morocco, Texas

Bio: Sure, my head is shaped a little differently than yours. The better to boomerang you with, my dear! I'm happy in my own skin. #onein251million #unique

**65 LOVES**

Look what I can do!  I'll use my own body as a #boomerang right . . . now!

 **DOUBLEDIPPER** #Ouch  #ThatHurt. I really need to stop doing that just to prove my point. 😥

**13**
photos

**721**
followers

**6,542**
following

Russ

Username: TANKSTERINO
Name: Scutosaurus (shield-reptile)
Period: Permian (299–252 million years ago)
Size: 10 feet long, heavy (like super, super heavy)
Diet: Plants
Hangouts: Russia
Bio: Don't I look like I would be fun to ride all around? Think again! I've got spikes along my skull to keep away hitchhikers #keepwalkin #cantridethistank

**30 LOVES**
#bigguy. When you're my size, you can't run too fast—but my #thickskin helps protect me from predators. #Takinmytime #everydayarmor

 **CAPTAIN_COOLIO** we'll see about that . . . see how my #BITES feel!

**1**
photos

**721**
followers

**1.2M**
following

Ever
Place
Ear

Username: XOTHEGREATDYINGXO

Name: The Permian Extinction

Period: 251 million years ago

Size: Hmm. I'm not sure how to describe my size, since I'm not exactly a single thing. I'm really more of an event. So . . . I don't know . . . I guess my size would be "the biggest die-off of all time"? I hope that helps!

Diet: Oh my gosh. I love food! Where to start, really? I love eati about 95 percent of all marine species and 70 percent of all terrestrial species alive in the Permian.

Hangouts: Earth #allmine #badsharer

Bio: Let's see . . . I LOVE volcanoes spewing toxic gas everywhe

**100 LOVES**

Don't cry because it's over. 😥 Smile because it's now time for the dinosaurs! 🙂

**PROMKING15** thank you. thank you for giving me an excuse to skip prom. #grateful

**13**
photos

**721**
followers

**6,542**
following

Texas

Username: LONESTARLIZARD

Name: Postosuchus

Period: Triassic (252–201 million years ago)

Size: 6.5 feet tall, 20 feet long

Diet: Meat! I'm a Texan after all!!

Hangouts: Texas, baby!

Bio: Go, Texas Longhorns! Shorthorns, too. Any of the #herbivores I like to eat, really. It's so fun to jump out at them and then chase them so that I can eat them. Woo-hoo!

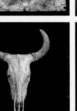

**30 LOVES**

#TEXASBABY! #LoneStarState. #DontMessWithTexas because now it's filled with #Humongous #Running crocodiles!

 **DOUBLEDIPPER** Yay Texas! #neighbors

 **LONESTARLIZARD** Didn't I just read you hurt yourself? #notscary #don'tmesswithyourself

35
photos

111
followers

264
following

Turkistan

Username: FEARLESSFLYER4EVER
Name: Longisquama (long-scales)
Period: Triassic (252–201 million years ago)
Size: 6 inches
Diet: Tinier insects
Hangouts: Turkistan
Bio: I'm all about living life on the edge. That's right! I'm a total daredevil. 😜 #noregrets #glideeveryday

**70 LOVES**
YOLO! #justjump

**CONCERNEDREPTILEPARENTS** How DARE you! How dare you encourage our children to glide a little bit as they jump between branches! 😠

**FEARLESSFLYER4EVER** I never said I was a #rolemodel. Now excuse me #whileikissthesky. #WHOOOOOOOOO 😎

**52** photos

**101** followers

**223** following

South weste United State

**Username:** DEZMAN1992
**Name:** Desmatosuchus
**Period:** Triassic (252–201 million years ago)
**Size:** 16 feet long
**Diet:** Plants on plants!
**Hangouts:** USA!
**Bio:** Sup! I'm Dez. Just a regular, reptile kind of guy with an upturned pig nose and a pair of back horns. I like movies, kickb and plants. #nomnomnom

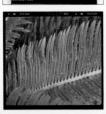

**16 LOVES**
Another day means another chance to use my
#backhorns. #DontLeaveHomeWithoutEm

 **SUPADUPAFLY** BTW, what do you actually use
them for? Always been curious about that.

 **DEZMAN1992** What DON'T I use them for is more
like it. #everything

 **SUPADUPAFLY** What specifically, though?

 **DEZMAN1992** Um. Like . . . to protect myself.
#dontmesswithme

1
photos

10
followers

0
following

Argent

Username: OLDMANHERRERASAURUS

Name: Herrerasaurus (Herrera's lizard)

Period: Triassic (231.4 million years ago)

Size: 4 feet tall, 13 feet long

Diet: Carnivore

Hangouts: Argentina

Bio: Greetings! Welcome to my official Internet web page. I am proud to be one of the first and oldest creatures called a "dinosaur."

#Greetings.

 **DINOOBSESSION** I am a seven-year-old and I LOVE dinosaurs. I would like to know what makes a dinosaur a dinosaur, though. Why is T. rex a dinosaur but Dimetrodon is not?

 **OLDMANHERRERASAURUS** For some reason, my message did not send. I pushed the button and instead of sending it, the message was erased. I hope this message goes through. Now I will type my message again. A dinosaur is a term that describes a large group of prehistoric reptiles with bodies that have many similarities.

**70**
photos

**2,164**
followers

**407**
following

Wales

Username: MILKYMORGAN

Name: Morganucodon

Period: Triassic to Jurassic (252–145 million years ago)

Size: 4 inches long, 1 ounce

Diet: Insects #slurp and other small animals

Hangouts: Wales, China

Bio: I'm one of the first mammals ever – I've got fur, I give birth live young (no strange old eggs), and I feed them with milk!

Mouse Milk

★ **51 LOVES**

Okay, I'm sorta #smalltime right now. But I've got big dreams! My kids love my milk, and I think everyone else will, too! #MouseMilkEmpire. #MouseMilk4All. #StayTuned. #ComingSoon to a #TriassicSupermarket near you.

 **#1_REPTILIA** That's right! Dream big! Work hard! Make that money!

 **SUPADUPAFLY** Does your mouse milk empire sell Muscle Milk? #getfit

**345** photos

**2,716** followers

**564** following

Germany

Username: NOODLENECKFISHING

Name: Tanystropheus (long-necked one)

Period: Triassic (252–201 million years ago)

Size: 20 feet long – 10 feet of which are my neck

Diet: Pescatarian #fisheater

Hangouts: Germany, Israel, Switzerland

Bio: I live for fishing! Let's just say I'm not a fan of #throwbackthursday – when I catch 'em, I eat 'em!

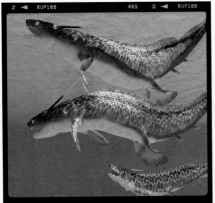

GONE FISHING

★ **541 LOVES**

Gone fishin' #viewsfordays

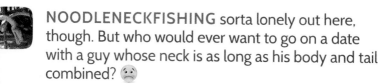

**NOODLENECKFISHING** sorta lonely out here, though. But who would ever want to go on a date with a guy whose neck is as long as his body and tail combined? 😢

**TANYSTRELLY_XO** Hey, @noodleneckfishing, my neck is as long as my body and tail combined!

**NOODLENECKFISHINGFANATIC** 😊

**125**
photos

**300**
followers

**175**
following

Pangea

**Username:** PANGEAPARTAY

**Name:** Pangea (all the Earth)

**Period:** Paleozoic to Mesozoic (200–50 million years ago)

**Size:** The biggest, most incredible continent party of all time!

**Hangouts:** Everywhere

**Bio:** For hundreds of millions of years, all the continents were smashed up against one another. It absolutely rocked.

#werockas1

## 24 LOVES

#RememberWhen @NorthAmerica @SouthAmerica @Europe @Asia @Australia @Antarctica

 **SOUTHAMERICA** HAH! AWESOME pic. I had a blast chilling with all y'all.

 **AFRICA** Couldn't agree more! 😢 Sad we had to go our separate ways, but I'll cherish the memories of this party forever. It was just that sick!!

 **NORTHAMERICA** Exactly! So why wait another 200 million years to do it again? Let's just all instantly smash back into one another.

**500** photos
**427** followers
**251** following

Great Britain

Username: COOLLILBRO
Name: Dimorphodon
Period: Jurassic (175–160 million years ago)
Size: 5 pounds, with a 4-foot wingspan
Diet: Fish and insects #greedy
Hangouts: Great Britain
Bio: I'm a lizard AND I'm an early pterosaur, which means "wing lizard." That's right, I can fly. Take THAT, @crocodiles. The only thing is I have just a touch of acrophobia. Oh, you don't know what that means? Um . . . well . . . it means I'm just the teeniest, tiniest bit afraid of heights.

⭐ **26 LOVES**

Nothin' to see up here. #TheGroundIsWhereIt'sAt

 **COOLOLDERBRO** Not this again! Dad said you're grounded if you keep telling people your secret! Dimorphodon up, bro!

**201** photos

**7,600** followers

**521** following

Colorado

Username: **POETASAURUS**

Name: **Stegosaurus ("Roof lizard")**

Period: **Jurassic (159–144 million years ago)**

Size: **30 feet long**

Diet: **Plants**

Hangouts: **Colorado, Utah, Wyoming #westisthebest**

Bio: **Big dino with big plates. But don't let my size trick you – my mind is the biggest thing about me! Brains > Muscles ppl!!**

⭐ **51 LOVES**

Yeah, yeah, yeah. Everybody always focuses on these #plates. Why not the #mind behind them? #smarts

 **MEGASTEGA** I thought our brains were the size of walnuts? 😕

 **STEGZ** Yeah, I always thought we had some of the smallest brains out of any dinosaurs.

 **POETASAURUS** Life lesson number one: you can't let anyone tell you what you can or can't do! Here's a poem I wrote about that very subject. It's called "Inspiration No. 1": Leaf. eat bark. swing tail. walk. eat. walk. walk around. eat leaf.

**425** photos

**707** followers

**24** following

Western Europe

Username: BIRDSRDINOS
Name: Archaeopteryx
Period: Jurassic (150–148 million years ago)
Size: 1 foot long
Diet: Smaller creatures #LookOutBelow
Hangouts: Western Europe
Bio: All eyes on me, kids! I have some real important news to drop. That's right, you are never going to BELIEVE what I have to tell you. I look sorta like a bird, right? Well #spreadtheword: #BirdsAreDinosaurs and #DinosaursAreBirds! THIS. CHANGES EVERYTHING.

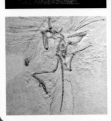

⭐ **200 LOVES**
I believe I can fly. #FlyingDino #BirdsAreDinosToo

**AFRIENDLYPALEONTOLOGIST** That's right, @BirdsRDinos! Birds are the last remaining line of dinosaurs! So dinosaurs still exist today!

**21STCENTURYPERSON** Okay, okay. Very interesting. But when you say "dinosaurs still exist," people think, you know, ACTUAL dinosaurs still exist. Like @Official_Rex1. Or @b_rachs_rox. So how about we put all that "dinosaurs still exist" stuff on hold for a little? Until we got some "real" dinosaurs on the scene again?

374
photos

2,340
followers

567
following

Portug[al]

Username: ALTHEKING
Name: Allosaurus ("Different lizard." That's right – different!)
Period: Jurassic (155–150 million years ago)
Size: I'm about the size of a T. rex. Okay, I'm a little smaller. But smaller is better! That means I'm faster than a T. rex. Probably li[ke] a hundred times faster. A million times faster!
Diet: Meat! And, hey, who's to say it wasn't . . . I don't know, T. re[x] meat? I mean, 150 million years is a really long time ago. How can we say with any certainty that I didn't eat T. rexes?
Hangouts: Portugal
Bio: So crazy different. #unique

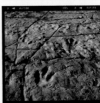

★ **10 LOVES**

#tbt to that time when I remembered I have #threefingers instead of boring old #two like @Official_Rex1. So #hilarious.

 **ALTHEKING** #crazy how much I can do with #threefingers that I couldn't do with two. 😬

 **OFFICIAL_REX1** Only 10 loves @Altheking? #nobodylikesaliar #watchyourtail

 **ALTHEKING** Who's the real king? Sound off in the comments, fans! #AlvsOfficial_Rex1

893
photos

642
followers

439
following

Afric

Username: B_RACHS_ROX

Name: Brachiosaurus ("Arm lizard." Yeah. I mean, it's not the coolest name ever, but it was my grandfather's!)

Period: Jurassic to Cretaceous (156–145 million years ago)

Size: 50 feet tall. 5-foot-long head. So, yeah. I'm like your hous If it had six floors. And a 5-foot-long head. And was a dinosaur.

Diet: Delicious leaves at the tops of cycad trees. OMG, so good. Eat some now!

Hangouts: North America, Africa

Bio: Seriously. Go do it. I can tell that you aren't eating a cycad l right now. I'm not going to continue until there's a big cycad lea your mouth, being chewed.

**51 LOVES**

Brontosaurus? Please. Turns out they never existed. I'm the #realdeal, though. One of the #tallestanimalsever. #WeatherUpHereIsNice #niceview

 **THEREALBRONTSTER88** I . . . don't even know what to say . . . I bought this book because I was excited to learn about my ancestors . . . But you're saying I'm not even real? 😢

 **B_RACHS_ROX** Shoot, man, I'm sorry. I totally wasn't thinking. It's okay, though – your real name is Apatosaurus.

**231**
photos

**652**
followers

**844**
following

Sou
Amer

Username: SCENETEENOSAURUS

Name: Amargasaurus

Period: Cretaceous (130 million years ago)

Size: 30 feet long, 4,000 pounds, infinity miles of back spikes

Diet: Plants

Hangouts: South America

Bio: You can look, but you can't touch. See my two rows of spik
down by my neck and back? They're taller than your spikes.
#spikelife. I #SufferForFashion

**73 LOVES**
Dinos may come and go, but my #PunkStyle will never die. #goth4life #sceneteen #emospikes #lookbutdoNOTtouch

**CAPTAIN_COOLIO** Sweet sails, bro!

**HAIRTIPSFORSHARKS** Hey! Get your own thing!

333
photos

629
followers

1,172
following

Egypt

Username: SPINOSAURUS1

Name: Spinosaurus

Period: Cretaceous (112–97 million years ago)

Size: 59 feet long, 22 tons, 6-foot-tall spines

Diet: Absolutely anything I want.

Hangouts: Egypt, Morocco

Bio: Yes, I'm deadly – as deadly as they come. But you know what? I keep it low-key. Why bring unwanted attention? I got a good thing going, and I don't wanna mess that up. #humble #blessed

**700 LOVES**

Lookin' good. #largestlandpredatorever. Yes, that means BIGGER than #ahem #coughcough #T_SomethingorOther. But you know what? I'm not jealous. I'm not in this for the fame.

 **OFFICIAL_REX1** Well put, my friend. You do a great job of showing how not jealous you are. #sarcasm

**256** photos

**78** followers

**2,921** following

Mongolia

Username: THEINFAMOUSVR
Name: Velociraptor
Period: Cretaceous (75–71 million years ago)
Size: About the size of a . . . let me just look in my "#historic" book about creatures from the future . . . Okay, about the size of a very large "chicken." I don't know what that is exactly, but I'm guessing it's a very large and scary monster.
Diet: All flesh, all the time.
Hangouts: Mongolia
Bio: Cretaceous's Most Wanted . . . perhaps you've heard of me. Even my name means "speedy thief." You may have heard of me, but you'll never see me. #badboy4lyfe

**81 LOVES**
Most people #KeepTheirDistance when they see me . . .
If only that were true of my little sister and her friends.
#SlumberPartyNight . . . #GetMeOuttaHere!

 **VELOCISISTER** Oh my gosh are you talking about us on here?! Just for that we're going to put some polish on your #RazorbladeClaws!!

 **THEINFAMOUSVR** No! Please! Leave me be!!

 **VELOCISISTER** After we paint those claws . . . maybe your #PrettyFeathers will need some braiding!!! #MWAHAHAHA #EvilLaughEvilLaugh

**121** photos

**3,321** followers

**629** following

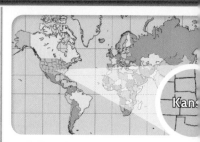

Kan

Username: IBITE

Name: Tylosaurus

Period: Late Cretaceous (88–80.5 million years ago)

Size: 40 feet long

Diet: Sharks, plesiosaurs, seabirds #whateverIfeellike

Hangouts: Kansas. When Kansas was underwater.

Bio: I'm a mosasaur: a giant, endlessly hungry lizard that lives in the sea. #DontCrossMe. And, yes, #iBite

**45 LOVES**
#Lunchstagram #RawPlesiosaurs #WithASideofSeabird

 **MUCHOMOSASAUR** Dude, you can't be posting pics like that . . . you could get in serious trouble.

 **IBITE** Yeah right. And how are they gonna pin these on me? If anyone asks, I'll just say it was photoshopped. #perfectcrime

 **TIMEPOLICE** @iBite, the citizens of the future have uncovered this fossil of you. A @Plesiosaur skull was found inside your stomach

 **IBITE** Uh-oh . . . @iBite2 did it!

**661** photos

**710** followers

**892** following

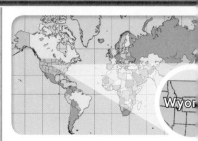

Wyo...

Username: KILLERSEAGIRAFFE22

Name: Elasmosaurus ("Thin-plated lizard." Please see below for more information on what to put on your plate to stay fit!)

Period: Cretaceous (145–66 million years ago)

Size: 46 feet long, 3 tons

Diet: Lean meat – but follow me for my secret, slimming tips!

Hangouts: Wyoming

Bio: I'm a plesiosaur – a long-necked swimming lizard. And I'd love to share some of my secret dieting tips with you! #Fit4Ly...

**16 LOVES**

Flexy Friday. #EatPebbles #PebblesHelpWithDigestion #PebblesOnTheOceanFloor #EatThem #MiraclePebblesDiet

 **KILLERSEAGIRAFFE22** Sorry for the spam, guys. I think I've been hacked by that "Eat Pebbles" virus that's been going around.

 **KILLERSEAGIRAFFE22** For the record, I do eat pebbles to aid in my digestion – that's why paleontologists find pebbles inside my fossils all the time.

**1,213**
photos

**443**
followers

**646**
following

Texas

Username: QUETZAKILLA

Name: Quetzalcoatlus

Period: Cretaceous (80–65 million years ago)

Size: 36-FOOT WINGSPAN. As tall as a giraffe!!

Diet: Most pterosaurs eat small fish. I eat large vertebrates – animals with spines.

Hangouts: Texas

Bio: I'm the biggest of all the pterosaurs. I was named after the Aztec god Quetzalcoatl. Because of my #UNBELIEVABLESIZE and #POWER and #FEROCITY. #FearMe

**1 LOVES**
Who else do you know that do it this big?
#SauropodSnacking

 **SUSANQUETZ** Honey, are you trying to be an Internet tough guy again? You don't need to do that, you know. We all love you for who you are – #sweet #sensitive #silly

 **QUETZAKILLA** MOM!!!! Get OUT of here!

 **SUSANQUETZ** Okay, okay! Sorry, sweetie. Lots of love to the biggest little guy I know! –Mommy P.S. Lots of kisses too!

846
photos

901
followers

732
following

Mongolia

Username: NOTHINGBUTNAILS
Name: Therizinosaurus (scythe lizard)
Period: Cretaceous (75–70 million years ago)
Size: Almost as big as a T. rex. But . . .
Diet: . . . I just eat plants even though I have 2-foot-long, unbelievably sharp claws.
Hangouts: Mongolia, Kazakhstan, Russia
Bio: If I could wish for anything, it would be for world peace. Can't we all just get along, @Official_Rex1? Nice guys finish first #bekind #grateful

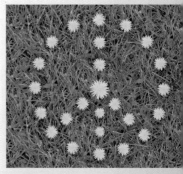

**22 LOVES**
Be kind to one another. #worldpeace
#DinosThatWorkTogetherStayTogether #equality
#QOTD

 **OFFICIAL_REX1** All dinos are not created equal.
#sorrynotsorry

**230**
photos

**461**
followers

**524**
following

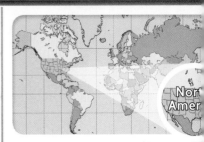

Nort
Amer

Username: DUCKFACEZ
Name: Parasaurolophus
Period: Cretaceous (76.5–73 million years ago)
Size: 40 feet tall with a 6-foot-tall crest
Diet: Devoted vegetarian. #meatkills
Hangouts: North America
Bio: #WeirdfactWednesday: behind my #duckbill, I've got thousands of teeth. Thousands! haha! How crazy is that?! #originalduckface

No – the #DuckFace is NOT just a pose for pictures! We use these babies (and the cool things on our heads) to communicate in the deep forests. And also because it's NEVER wrong to #DuckFace. #CantStopWontStop

**HAIRTIPSFORSHARKS** Hi there! Ignore my user name! Everyone's hair needs a little love! Check out my page to found out how to handle that do!

**561**
photos

**251**
followers

**263**
following

Sout
Dako

Username: NEATOTURTLITO

Name: Archelon

Period: Cretaceous (100–66 million years ago)

Size: About the length of 12 foot-long rulers laid end to end, ar
roughly the width of 16 foot-long rulers also laid end to end. I
wonder if there's an easier way to say that . . .

Diet: Squid squid squid.  #CanIHaveThisFried? #calamari

Hangouts: South Dakota, Wyoming

Bio: Biggest turtle of all time. #OhYeahBaby!

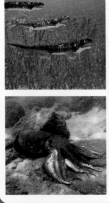

**58 LOVES**

Fell asleep on the ocean floor and then #IWokeUpLikeThis. Just in time for #FossilFriday!

**NOTHINGBUTNAILS** You look so #peaceful

**299**
photos

**443**
followers

**2,008**
following

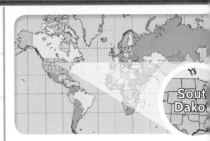

Sout
Dako

Username: BONEDOMESMASHER
Name: Pachycephalosaurus
Period: Cretaceous (72–66 million years ago)
Size: 16 feet long, 950 pounds. Big head dome, good for smash
Diet: Smash plants with mini bone domes inside mouth. Smash
smash smash. Smash smash smash. Swallow swallow swallow.
Hangouts: Montana, Wyoming, South Dakota
Bio: Have bone dome on head. Fun to smash. Lives in herds. Li
to smash head on friends.

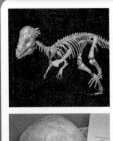

★ **300 LOVES**
Welcome to the dome zone. #smashbrothers

 **KILLERSEAGIRAFFE22** Hey there! I saw that you're in the Cretaceous period. I just moved in here! What do you guys do for fun?

 **BONEDOMESMASHER** #domesmash 😬

 **KILLERSEAGIRAFFE22** I'm sorry?

 **BONEDOMESMASHER** #smashdome

**245** photos

**3,972** followers

**6,158** following

New Mexico

**Username:** PENTACERA45
**Name:** Pentaceratops (five-horned face)
**Period:** Cretaceous (75–73 million years ago)
**Size:** 20 feet, 8 tons
**Diet:** All the plants I can get my beak on
**Hangouts:** New Mexico
**Bio:** I'm a father first, husband second, and ceratopsian third. Family is the most important thing to me in the world.
#AllYouNeedIsLove

**50 LOVES**

Home-improvement day! Working on a brand-new nest for @MrsPentacera and our soon-to-be-laid #ClutchOfEggs. #StepOne: Soften some of the ground up with my beak.

 **PENTACERA45** Hmm . . . those horns are stuck in there #realgood. #shoot.

 **@MRSPENTACERA** That's okay, pookieceras, it's the thought that counts. <3 #StillLoveYou #4lyfe #LittleHelp, people? #LittleHelp.

 **PENTACERA45** Oh, why do all my #homeimprovementprojects have to end this way?

**506** photos

**12,600** followers

**7,916** following

Gobi Desert

Username: FLEETFOOT23

Name: Gallimimus (rooster mimic)

Period: Cretaceous (70 million years ago)

Size: 20 feet long, 6 feet off the ground (best way to practice a proper running stance)

Diet: Herbivorous. Because achieving your best time isn't just about working out – it's about eating right, too. #eatclean

Hangouts: Gobi Desert

Bio: I guess you could say I'm a speed freak. Translation? Runnin is my passion. I pursue excellence every day. I run this desert.

#ItWasAllABlur

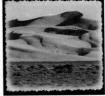

★ 801 LOVES

Hit #30to40mph today while training. Feeling unbelievable. #crushingit #fartherfasterstronger #instafit #workouttime #catchup

 **PROTOCERATOPSMOMMY** Is it normal to feel bad about myself whenever I look at your feed? 😢

 **FLEETFOOT23** Yes.

**222**
photos

**0**
followers

**1.3M**
following

United States

Username: OFFICIAL_REX1

Name: Tyrannosaurus rex. (In the process of changing my name to Tyrockstarosaurus Rexington. #rebranding)

Period: Cretaceous (68–65 million years ago. Kickin' back for the last 66 million years – and still the most famous dino!)

Size: Huge. Gigantic. Colossal.

Diet: I kill stuff and eat it. I find dead stuff and eat it. #special.

Hangouts: USA, Canada, Mongolia, TV, Internet, Movies

Bio: Yo, @triceratops, I'm really happy for you, and I'll let you finish, but I had the best photo of all time! Even my name means "king!" Everybody's scared of me cuz I'm the biggest carnivore around. Just one thing, why won't anyone follow me?!

★ **0 LOVES**

Anybody out there? I'll find you. #selfiesunday

**PLESIOSAURUS** @official_rex1, not me! T. rexes can't swim LOL!!

**OFFICIAL_REX1** Guess you've never seen my #dinopaddle. Here I come @Plesiosaurus!

**PLESIOSAURUS** AHHHHHHHHHHHHHHHHHHHHHHHHHHHH!!!!

**222**
photos

**0**
followers

**1.3M**
following

Canada

Username: SLOWANDSTEADY

Name: Euoplocephalus ("Well-armored head." Could it be any lamer? Why can't I have some cool name?)

Period: Cretaceous (76.5–75.6 million years ago)

Size: 20 feet long, two tons

Diet: Roots and tubers

Hangouts: Canada

Bio: I'm a member of the Ankylosaurus family. We're all covered in bony plates and have these tails that are like clubs. Trust me, sounds cooler than it is. It's only there because we're too big and slow to run away from our predators.

**58 LOVES**

#selfie #ew #bulkcentral #lumpytail #imsogigantic #awkward

 **NOTHINGBUTNAILS** NOOOOO. You are GORGEOUS!!!!

 **SLOWANDSTEADY** haha ur way too nice . . . no need to lie to me, though, know i'm #spiky and #ugly . . . and these bone plates are like #gross. 😢

 **NOTHINGBUTNAILS** OMG! QUIT IT! You're SOOOO gorgeous #loveyourself

1
photos

0
followers

1M
following

World
wide

**Username:** CRETACEOUSDEATHSTORM
**Name:** The Cretaceous–Paleogene Extinction, aka the K–Pg extinction
**Period:** 66 million years ago
**Diet:** 80% of all species
**Hangouts:** Worldwide
**Bio:** Let's just cut to the chase here: I'm kind of the party pooper. The dinosaurs had their time. On to the next one! #yolo

**92 LOVES**

#massivecomet with the energy of #onebillionnukes. #dustcloud so large that it covers the sun for a year. #ByeByeDinos

 **OFFICIAL_REX1** Hey, hey, hey! Just heard that there might be some sort of cataclysmic #extinctionevent! Wow, I hate to be #thatguy, but I was wondering – any chance I could get a little, you know, #startreatment? 😎

 **CRETACEOUSDEATHSTORM** Well . . . why not? Come stand over here . . . yep, right in that spot, very nice . . . Stay nice and still . . . and now look up at that "star" in the sky. Enjoy!

272
photos

6,417
followers

1,023
following

Sout
Ameri

Username: THEREALBIGBIRD

Name: Phorusrhacid ("Scar-bearer." But all my friends just call n #terrorbird)

Period: Paleocene to Pleistocene (4.9–1.8 million years ago)

Size: 10 feet tall

Diet: Meeeaaat

Hangouts: South America, North America

Bio: Big Bird? Great guy, great guy. But let's just say I'm gonna b
the #NextBigThing. I can kung fu kick. Did that yellow guy ever
that?

🔖 51 LOVES

#ReadyForMyCloseup! I'm just like your favorite fluffy yellow guy. But I'm #10FeetTall. And #DeadlyFast. With a beak that'll cut you in half.

THEREALBIGBIRD In other words, how can you NOT make me the star of a show for three- and four-year-olds?

| 101 | photos |
| 631 | followers |
| 812 | following |

Trop
of So
Ame

**Username:** CUDDLYCONSTRICTOR

**Name:** Titanoboa ("Titanic boa." Like, maybe a larger version of my cousin the boa constrictor, I guess. But what if that "boa" is actually there to make you think of bows? Like pretty bows wrapped around beautiful presents I got for you!)

**Period:** Paleocene (60–58 million years ago)

**Size:** 42 feet long, 2,500 pounds – of friendship 😐

**Diet:** Weird question! LOL! Come on, who cares?! It's not like w I eat is weird or scary or anything. Let's just move on.

**Hangouts:** Tropics of South America

**Bio:** Ha-ha, come on, enough about me already! Let's talk abo you. You're in need of a hug, aren't you?

**201 LOVES**

#JustOneOfThoseDays . . . You know, the kind where you're #InNeedOfAHug? You're my friend, right? Waddya say? Hug it out?

 **CUDDLYCONSTRICTOR** LOL, no responses . . . #Really? I promise this isn't a way to trick you into being squeezed to death and eaten by me.

 **CUDDLYCONSTRICTOR** Srsly, nobody? #WasItSomethingISaid?

**22** photos
**764** followers
**981** following

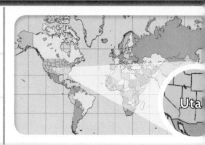

Uta

Username: FANTASTICFURREDFLYER
Name: Icaronycteris (Icarus night flyer)
Period: Eocene (55–34 million years ago)
Size: Roughly the size of a small, flying rodent.
Diet: Insects. Like, flying ones. In the air. And I'm in the air, too. Flying. But I'm not a bird! I'm a mammal! Can you believe that? I'm basically like . . . a flying dog!
Hangouts: Colorado, Wyoming, Utah
Bio: Totally unbelievable beast. I might as well be out of some science fiction story. I mean – a flying mammal. You're a mammal, right?! So actually, I'm like a flying YOU.

**7 LOVES**

#faroutfriday #mammal . . . but #IBelieveICanFly. The question is, CAN YOU believe it?

**AFRIENDLYPALEONTOLOGIST** Sure we can! You are an ancestor of modern-day bats – flying mammals that everyone knows! In fact, you look a ton like those modern bats.

**FANTASTICFURREDFLYER** But can these amazing "modern-day bats" of yours find their food through echolocation?

**AFRIENDLYPALEONTOLOGIST** That is a great question! Yes, they can.

101
photos

299
followers

3,171
following

Plains of
Mongolia

Username: CARNIVORIAGLORIA

Name: Andrewsarchus

Period: Eocene (45–36 million years ago)

Size: 13 feet long, 2,000 pounds, appetite for days

Diet: Meat, meat, meat. And did I happen to mention: meat? C
yes. Yes, I did. Well, why not do it one more time, then? MEAT!

Hangouts: Mongolian Plains

Bio: I'm Gloria. But you can just call me The Giant, Long-Heade
Dog-Looking Thing That's About To Eat You.

**51 LOVES**

#meatlessmondays? Yeah, right. How about . . .
#MeatMOREMondays! Or #EatMoreMeatMoreMondays
. . . um . . . #more. #meat. #eatsome. Fine, so I'm
not the greatest hashtag creator ever. But I AM the
#TopCarnivore of the Eocene!  #illeat2that

**THEREALBIGBIRD** LOL! Right on
@Carnivoriagloria I love meat, too. Wanna meat,
I mean meet for dinner? #it'snotadate

**12**
photos

**465**
followers

**912**
following

Plains of
Asia

Username: SLAMMAJAMMAMAMMA

Name: Indricotherium

Period: Oligocene to Miocene (30 to 16.6 million years ago)

Size: 40 feet long, 40,000 pounds

Diet: To stay on top, I eat #AnUnbelievableAmountOfLeaves Everyday.

Hangouts: The plains of Asia

Bio: I'm the biggest land mammal that ever lived – in fact, nea as big as some of the guys in the Brachiosaurus family. Perfect #BasketballDomination!

**51 LOVES**

#SheShootsSheScores! #SlammaJammaExtraordinaire!
#TheBestThereIs! Now if only anyone else in prehistory
played basketball. #Sigh. Maybe I'll #TakeMyTalents to
the #Future.

 **SUPADUPAFLY** You're ripped
@slammajammamamma! #fitness

 **NOODLENECKFISHING** I'm tall. I can ball.
Pick me!

| | |
|---|---|
| **10** photos | |
| **201** followers | |
| **760** following | |

The Plains of Eurasia

**Username:** MOROPUSOBSESSED

**Name:** Moropus

**Period:** Miocene (23–13.6 million years ago)

**Size:** 10 feet tall. One ton. Style for days.

**Diet:** I eat plants. Just like @Moropus3!!!! We have so much in common! <3 <3

**Hangouts:** The plains (and runways) of Eurasia

**Bio:** You guys! How cute is @Moropus3? He is just so dreamy. That's why I started this page with all of his best photos. #marryme #junewedding

MOROPUS

**67 LOVES**

Man crush Monday. How adorable is @Moropus3 just walking on his knuckles? Horse + Gorilla = moropus. 🐴 #MCM

**MOROPUS3** Aw Shucks.

**MOROPUSOBSESSED** OMG!! You spoke to me! #dying

301
photos

291
followers

146
following

Africa

Username: SHOVELEPHANT
Name: Platybelodon
Period: Miocene (15–4 million years ago)
Size: 9 feet tall with a big ol' flop-o mouth
Diet: Sweet, sweet bark, which my mouth is designed to scrape off. Man, I'm getting hungry just THINKING about that bark!
Hangouts: Africa, Europe, Asia, North America
Bio: One of many different species of prehistoric elephant – but I'm the ONLY one who's got an insane #ShovelMouth. #winnin

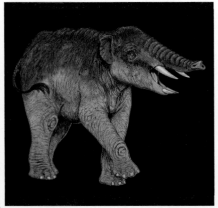

**67 LOVES**

How are YOU celebrating #NationalShovelMouthDay??
#LIKE this picture if you're duct-taping a shovel onto your
face. #COMMENT if you're forcing your parents to get
you some braces that stretch your mouth to the ground
and give you two #BuckTeeth.

**DUCKFACEZ** That's a pretty good face, but not as
pretty as #duckface!

200
photos

121
followers

646
following

Per

**Username:** SURFERSLOTHMAXIMUS
**Name:** Thalassocnus (sea sloth)
**Period:** Miocene to Pliocene (10–2 million years ago)
**Size:** 6 feet long, 500 pounds, chill for days
**Diet:** Seagrass, seaweed, seaburgers (a super-chill species of #LivingHamburger during the Miocene that all the chilliest water-dwelling prehistoric creatures ate)
**Hangouts:** Peru, Chile, Coastin' Down South America
**Bio:** What's cooler than being a super-chill sloth? #nothing! How about a super-chill giant prehistoric swimming sloth? #evenMOREnothing!!

**43 LOVES**
Catchin some waves #chillin #seaside #SlothStyle

 **CHILLPREHISTORICJELLYFISH** Sup, g! You wanna come over to 500 million years ago and chill?

 **SURFERSLOTHMAXIMUS** 😎 #ButOfCourse.

 **SURFERSLOTHMAXIMUS** (To all my human buddies reading this, I forgot to mention that in addition to living seaburgers, another thing that went extinct was living, swimming time machines. They're so fun. Don't you guys agree?)

**760** photos

**491** followers

**326** following

Sou
Amer

Username: TINYTRUNKSRCOOL

Name: Macrauchenia (long llama)

Period: Miocene to Pleistocene (7 million–10 thousand years a

Size: 10 feet long with a nose that's sorta like a dangling Slinky

Diet: Do you know how many plants I can eat with this thing?

Hangouts: South America

Bio: Mom says my trunk gives me character. Shout-out to all r buddies in the herd! #socialcreature

**67 LOVES**
What a great day with my BFF! #7MillionHappyYears
#Year1

 **SHOVELEPHANT** What kind of trunk is that?
#where'stheshovel

| 0 |
| photos |
| 0 |
| followers |
| 0 |
| following |

Nort
Amer

Username: UNDERGROUNDCRAFTS

Name: Ceratogaulus

Period: Miocene (10–5 million years ago)

Size: 1 gophersworth + 1 hornsworth

Diet: Roots, insects, and any number of delicious appetizers yo
can make yourself!

Hangouts: Woodlands of North America

Bio: Okay, so my name means "horned gopher" and, yes, I spe
a lot of time digging. But that's not my only hobby! I love to
#CRAFT, and I thought I'd share my passions with the world!

⭐ 67 LOVES

#CraftOfTheDay: a hole to live inside! First #dig in the dirt with your #longclaws to make a burrow. Now, use your #horns as a #partyhat to celebrate your new home! #cozy #DIY #artsandcrafts

 **AFRIENDLYPALEONTOLOGIST** Beautiful pictures! Now, what if you don't have horns or claws? Can you still do #artsandcrafts?

 **UNDERGROUNDCRAFTS** No.

**52**
photos

**1,232**
followers

**3,764**
following

Username: MRSABERTOYOU

Name: Smilodon

Period: Pleistocene (2.6 million years ago–11,700 years ago)

Size: About the size of a lion, but heavier

Diet: Sloths, horses, and, camels, oh my!

Hangouts: South America

Bio: Everyone says I'm a tiger, but really I'm a cat. Don't get it twisted. You don't want to mess with this pet! Have you seen these teeth? #catnottiger

You're gonna hear me roar! #20inchteeth

 **BIGWOOLLYSTYLES** You call those things big? My tusks are 17 feet long.

 **MRSABERTOYOU** That's the only thing big about you, @BigWoollyStyles. You're only as big as an African elephant. haha! #notamammoth

**701**
photos

**2,220**
followers

**3,120**
following

Europe

**Username:** BIGWOOLLYSTYLES
**Name:** Woolly Mammoth
**Period:** Pliocene (5 million–4,500 years ago)
**Size:** Slightly smaller than modern elephants
**Diet:** Birch trees, grasses, sedges
**Hangouts:** Europe, Africa, Asia, North America
**Bio:** Hi, lady woollys. I'm single and lookin'! I may have put on a little #winterweight but I'm nowhere near MAMMOTH like some people say. I'm a lean, mean, adorable machine! Let's take a walk on the ice!

**★ 67 LOVES**

Class picture ready. #goodhairday #pearlywhitetusks

**SHOVELEPHANT** Lookin' good! Love those tusks. You're totally going to win best smile in the yearbook. #winning

**121** photos

**300** followers

**237** following

North America

Username: SPORTYBEAV
Name: Castoroides
Period: Pliocene to Pleistocene (3 million–10,000 years ago)
Size: As long as the tallest human who ever lived. Not bad for a beaver, I must say.
Diet: Reeds and grasses – breakfast of champions!
Hangouts: North America
Bio: I live for competition!

TEAM RODENT

⭐ 51 LOVES

Go #TeamRodent! Come by the GIANT NORTH AMERICAN PREHISTORIC MAMMALS CHAMPIONSHIP and watch me compete. I'll be in two events: my specialty, the Tree Eating Competition, and some other event called the Giant Beaver Being Eaten By Saber Tooth Cat Competition. I'm not sure why the second one is called that, and honestly, I don't have time to do any research about it at all. Well, I'm off to the games! #TeamRodentFTW!

 **MILKYMORGON** Mammals unite! You should try some #mousemilk for a balanced breakfast. #goodluck

**2,461**
photos

**10,300**
followers

**5,172**
following

Southe...
Russi...

Username: **DAPARTYBEAST**

Name: Elasmotherium (thin-plate monster)

Period: Pleistocene (2.5 million–50,000 years ago)

Size: 26 feet long – with a 6.5 foot horn! YEAH! WE DO IT BIG AROUND HERE!

Diet: Oh, man – all the tastiest grass, 24/7. Having a sick giant horn like this – it's not just fun and games all the time. Like, it's heavy and stuff! And people always want to touch it. So, yeah, I reward myself with the most delicious grass.

Hangouts: Southern Russia, Siberia

Bio: I'm an ancient rhinoceros – but just because I'm old doesn't mean I can't throw down! You think different? Tell it to the horn!

⭐ **26 LOVES**

Hitting the town tonight rocking the #FreshestHorn that's #tallerthanyourdad. #partyallthetime

 **BIGWOOLLYSTYLES** Dunno, dude . . . you might wanna chill on that. Like now that humans are on the scene we might just wanna keep a low profile . . . they seem #madextincty.

 **DAPARTYBEAST** Pssh. Have fun with that. I'm gonna #keepthepartygoing. 😜

**272** photos
**891** followers
**342** following

South America

Username: SAFETYFIRST

Name: Glyptodon

Period: Pliocene to Pleistocene (2.5 million years ago to 10,000 years ago)

Size: 10 feet long, 2,000 pounds, one big shell

Diet: Grass, good old nonthreatening, nondangerous grass

Hangouts: South America

Bio: Even though it might not be "#cool" or "#hip" or "a #GoodWayToMakeFriends," be like me and always wear a helm A full-body helmet covering almost every inch of your flesh. At times.

⭐ **112 LOVES**

Remember: it's dangerous out there! #Safetyfirst!!

 **TANKSTERINO**  Awesome helmet man! That looks newer than mine. #Jealous

**217**
photos

**445**
followers

**631**
following

Australia

**Username**: LIZARDFROMOZ
**Name**: Megalania (giant roamer)
**Period**: Pleistocene to Modern (2 million–30,000 years ago)
**Size**: 25 feet long, 4,000 pounds
**Diet**: Anything! Not a #PickyEater. I mean, as long as it's a #GiantPrehistoricMarsupial, I'm happy.
**Hangouts**: Australia #LandDownUnder, baby!
**Bio**: G'day, mates! I'm an unbelievably giant meat-eating lizard from the #LandDownUnder!

**71 LOVES**

Time for a little #Q&A! What do YOU want to know about living in the past as a giant prehistoric creature? #AskAway #LizardTipTuesday

 **SOCCER4LIFE2002** You're in Australia, right?

 **LIZARDFROMOZ** Yep! I was around when you guys first got here, in fact!

 **SOCCER4LIFE2002** Cool, cool. So do the toilets really run backward down there?

**100**
photos

**6.2B**
followers

**20M**
following

Northern India

Username: GIANTAPEQUESTIONS

Name: Gigantopithecus (Giant Ape)

Period: Miocene to Pleistocene (9 million–100,000 years ago)

Size: About 2 gorillas stacked together

Diet: Bamboo

Hangouts: Northern India, China

Bio: Not all #GiantApes are #KingKongs. #LoverNotAFighter #smarterthanyouraveragegorilla

★ **150 LOVES**

Here I am. In my #naturalhabitat. It's #peaceful and #serene in these mountain ranges.

 **HUMAN** That seems like a nice place to live . . .

PALEOZOIC ERA

MILLIONS OF YEARS AGO

550

### Cambrian Period
### 542–488 mya
### Age of Marine Invertebrates
First organisms with shells or external skeletons appear. Oceans full of creatures including brachiopods, which resemble modern-day clams, and arthropods, which are ancestors of insects, spiders, and crustaceans. Primitive corals and fish develop.

500

450

### Silurian Period
### 443–416 mya
### Rise of Land Animals
Jawed fish, evolved corals, and sponges appear. First true land plants emerge. Millipedes, some six feet long, and early spiders and mites creep onto land.

400

350

### Carboniferous Period
### 360–300 mya
### Rise of Reptiles
Development of amniotic egg allows early reptiles to inhabit and reproduce on land. Plentiful vegetation leads to an increase in oxyge in the atmosphere. Six-foot-long centipedes and three-foot-long cockroaches roam the growing forests. Amphibians also grow in size Winged insects take to the air.

300

250

PALEOZOIC ERA

550

500

450

400

350

300

250

MILLIONS OF YEARS AGO

### Ordovian Period
### 488–443 mya
### Rise of the Fish

Sea life triples and includes trilobites, who are the earliest-known animal to have vision, nautiloids that look like squids, and eels with backbones, called conodonts. Horseshoe crabs crawl onto land. Primitive corals and fish develop.

### Devonian Period
### 416–360 mya
### Age of Fishes / Rise of Amphibians

Ancestors to sharks and rays called cartilaginous fish thrive in oceans. Amphibious creatures called tetrapods, develop from bony fishes, ancestors of all four-limbed land vertebrates. Primitive insects arrive on the scene. First plants with roots emerge.

### Permian Period
### 300–250 mya
### Reptilian Diversification

Early reptiles—therapsids—split to become carnivores or herbivores, some sporting "sails" on their backs to collect heat from the sun. Seas are full with scaled bony fishes. Roaches, termites, and bees develop.

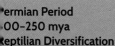

**PALEOZOIC ERA**

250

**MESOZOIC ERA**

200

MILLIONS OF YEARS AGO

150

100

**CENOZOIC ERA**
Tertiary Period

50

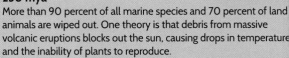

### The Permian Extinction
**250 mya**
More than 90 percent of all marine species and 70 percent of land animals are wiped out. One theory is that debris from massive volcanic eruptions blocks out the sun, causing drops in temperature and the inability of plants to reproduce.

### Triassic Period
**250-200 mya**
**Age of Reptiles**
Reptiles that survive the Permian Extinction develop into the first dinosaurs. Some rise off four feet into upright postures; others become the first flying reptiles, called pterosaurs. The earliest true mammal, a shrewlike creature that gives birth to live young, appears. Amphibious creatures flourish, including primitive crocodiles.

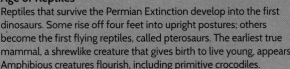

### Cretaceous Period
**144-65 mya**
**Dinosaur Shifts**
New species of dinosaurs appear as older ones settle in specific northern or southern climatological areas, some forming herds. Frogs, turtles, and snakes occupy the coastlines. Sharks resemble those of modern day. Primitive birds quickly acquire distinctive characteristics. Flowering plants, including grasses and hardwood trees, appear. Butterflies, moths, beetles, and ants thrive.

PALEOZOIC ERA

250

MESOZOIC ERA

### ?angea
### 70–200 mya
### ?ontinental Shifts

angea, a mash-up of all our present-day continents created by
?ovement of Earth's tectonic plates, begins to split up. The breakup
f Pangea over the course of time leads both to extinctions and
?evelopments of plant and animal species.

200

MILLIONS OF YEARS AGO

### ?urassic Period
### ?00–144 mya
### ?inosaur Domination

?inosaurs become more numerous and more diversified. Oceans
?warm with huge plesiosaurs, giant crocodiles and sharks, and
?ny plankton. Earliest known bird, *Archaeopteryx*, flies alongside
?terosaurs. Small early mammals the size of rats live among
?bundant plant life.

150

100

### ?he Cretaceous-Paleogene Extinction
### ?5 mya

?inosaurs and most land animals under 55 pounds become extinct
?etween the Cretaceous and Paleogene Periods. Scientists still
?ebate the cause, but agree that debris blocks out sunlight and
?estroys plant life on land and in the seas. One theory claims this
?as once again caused by massive volcanic activity. Another theory
?uggests that a giant asteroid or comet hit Earth.

CENOZOIC ERA
Tertiary Period

50

**CENOZOIC ERA**
Tertiary Period

MILLIONS OF YEARS AGO

50

40

30

20

### Eocene Epoch
### 56–34 mya
### Odd-Toes and Even-Toes
Two new groups of hoofed animals called ungulates appear: odd-toed like horses, rhinoceroses, and tapirs, and even-toed like deer, cattle, and sheep. First appearances of modern whales, porpoises, and dolphins, and primitive manatees and dugongs. Primitive elephants and bats develop.

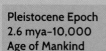

### Miocene Epoch
### 23–5 mya
### Primate Explosion
Higher primates, including apes and gibbons, are recorded, and distinguished from the lower primates like lemurs, lorises, and tarsiers. Land-dwelling mammals are essentially modern. Bears, hyenas, and saber-tooth cats, and primitive giraffes, seals, and walruses appear. Archaic elephants spread from Africa to Asia. Birds fly over all continents.

**CENOZOIC ERA**
Quaternary Period

10

### Pleistocene Epoch
### 2.6 mya–10,000
### Age of Mankind
Long-horned bison, giant ground sloths, horses, camels, mammoth and other large land mammals flourish in North America, all of whic go extinct by the end of the epoch. The human species appears.

**CENOZOIC ERA**
Tertiary Period

### aleocene Epoch
### 5–56 mya
### ge of Mammals

ontinents are almost in their present position. The first whales
ppear, the descendants of land mammals. Woodlands and
rasslands grow, as do herds of grazing hoofed mammals. "Archaic"
orms of dogs, cats, rats, and rabbits appear. In tropical and
ubtropical areas, early primates develop rotating shoulder joints,
hree-dimensional vision, and hands that can grasp.

50

40

### ligocene Epoch
### 4–23 mya
### hort but Sweet

Mammals continue to diversify and specialize. First recorded
ppearance of camels and pigs. Earliest apelike animals and New
World monkeys appear.

30

20

### liocene Epoch
### .3–2.6 mya
### etting Back Together

he North and South American continents are reconnected.
nimals known only in South America–ground sloths–armadillos,
possums, and porcupines now appear in North America. Woolly
hammoths and mastodons roam through all landmasses. The first
ominids–*australopithecines*–appear. The most recent glaciation
ce age) begins.

**CENOZOIC ERA**
Quaternary Period

10

MILLIONS OF YEARS AGO